fraction fun

David A. Adler

illustrated by Nancy Tobin

HOUGHTON MIFFLIN　　BOSTON

Fraction Fun, by David A. Adler, illustrated by Nancy Tobin. Text copyright © 1996 by David A. Adler. Illustrations copyright © 1996 by Nancy Tobin. All rights reserved. Reprinted by permission of Holiday House, Inc.

Copyright © by Houghton Mifflin Company. All rights reserved.

No part of this work may be reproduced or transmitted in any form or by any means, electronic or mechanical, including photocopying or recording, or by any information storage or retrieval system without the prior written permission of the copyright owner unless such copying is expressly permitted by federal copyright law. With the exception of nonprofit transcription into Braille, Houghton Mifflin is not authorized to grant permission for further uses of this work. Permission must be obtained from the individual copyright owner as identified herein. Address requests for permission to make copies of Houghton Mifflin material to School Permissions, Houghton Mifflin Company, 222 Berkeley Street, Boston, MA 02116.

Printed in the U.S.A.

ISBN: 0-618-43610-3

7 8 9 10-0920-13 12 11 10

A fraction is a part of something.

We use fractions all the time.

When someone says
she is eight and a half years old,
she is using a fraction.
She is saying that she is a fraction,
a part, of a year, more than eight.

When you share a granola bar
with a friend, you are using fractions, too.
Each of you is getting only a fraction,
a part, of the bar.

I'm twenty-one and a half... (in dog years)

Each time you eat a slice of pizza,
you are eating a fraction, a part, of the pie.

Most often pizza pies are cut into 8 slices,
into 8 equal parts.
Each slice is 1 of those 8 equal parts.
Each slice is one eighth (1/8) of the pie.

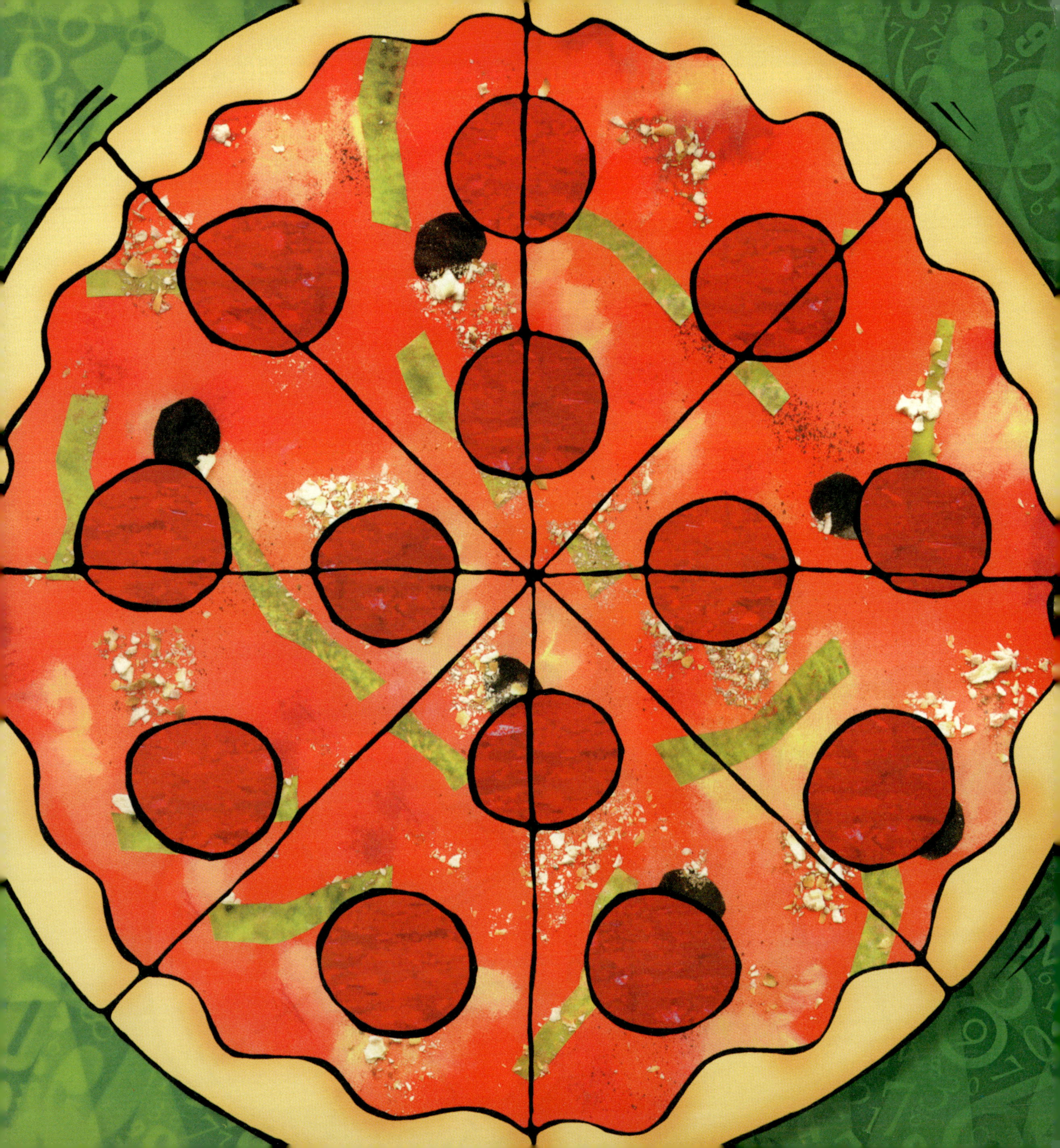

If you eat one slice, you are eating 1/8 of the pie.

If you eat 2 slices, you are eating 2/8 of the pie.
You are eating 2 of 8 equal parts.

1/8

← numerator

↙ denominator

In the fraction 1/8, the top number, the 1, is the "numerator."

The bottom number is the "denominator."

Each fraction has a numerator and a denominator, a top number and a bottom number.

Now let's do some

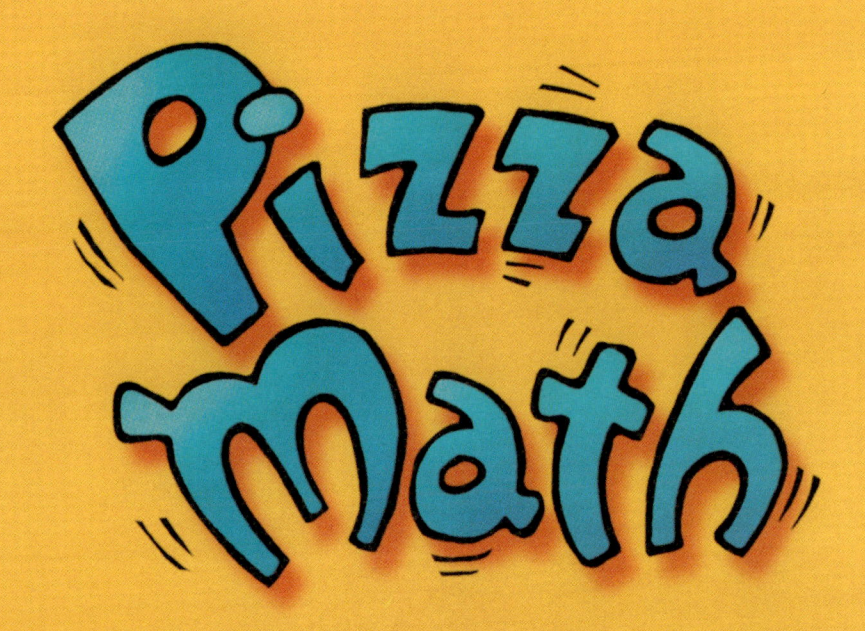

Pizza Math

It will teach you about fractions.

To do pizza math you will need:

three paper plates, all the same size,   a pencil,   a ruler,   and red, green, and blue crayons.

With the pencil,
mark the center of each plate.

Using the ruler,
draw a straight line through
the mark from one edge
of the plate to the other.

The lines you drew divided
each plate into 2 equal parts.
Each part is 1/2 of the plate.

If on your plates one part
is larger than the other,
it is probably because
your marks were not in the
exact centers of the plates.

On one plate, write "1/2"
in each of the two parts.
With the red crayon,
shade in 1 part,
1/2 of the plate.

On another plate, draw a second line from one edge to the other and through the center mark. Draw it so you divide the plate into 4 equal parts. Each part is 1/4 of the plate.

Write "1/4" in each of the four parts of the plate. With the red crayon, shade in 1 part, 1/4 of the plate.

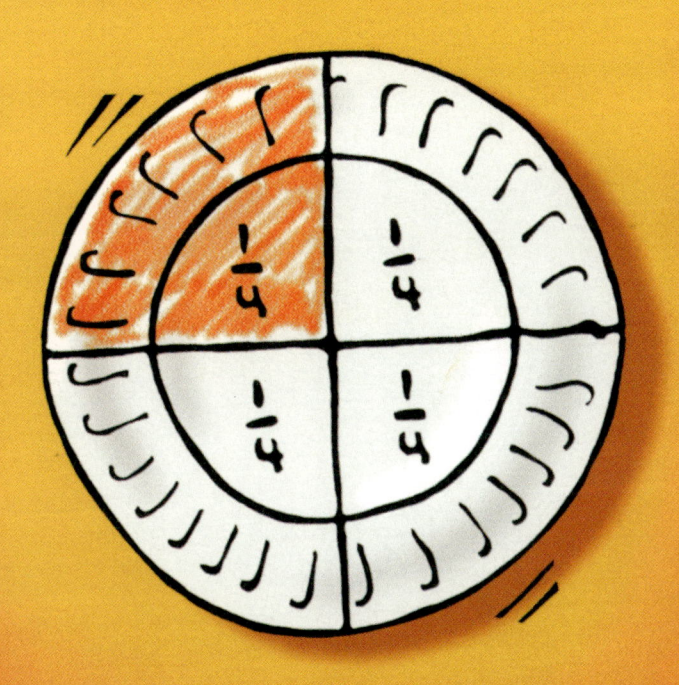

On the third plate, draw a second line through the center of the plate, dividing it into 4 equal parts. Next, draw two more lines through the center of the plate, dividing it into a total of 8 equal parts. Each part is 1/8 of the plate.

Write "1/8" in each of the eight parts of the plate. With the red crayon shade in 1 part, 1/8 of the plate.

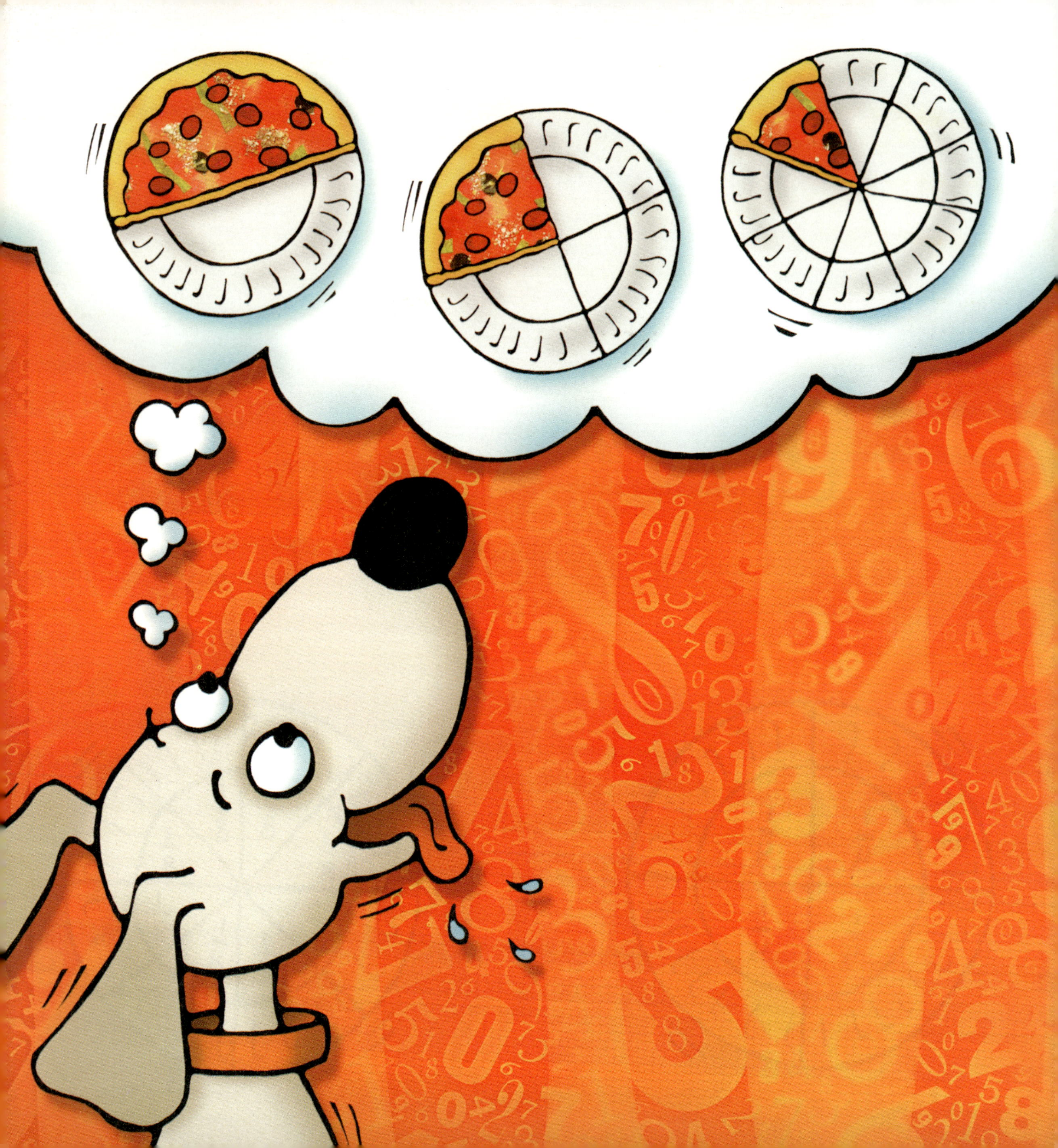

Now look at the three plates.
Pretend each of the plates is a pizza pie.
Pretend each red section is a slice of pizza.

Which slice is the largest, 1/2, 1/4, or 1/8?

Which slice is the smallest?

What happens to a fraction as the denominator,
the bottom number, changes?

As the denominator gets larger,
the fraction gets smaller.

As you cut the pie into more and more slices,
each pizza slice gets smaller and smaller.

With the green crayon shade in 2 sections of the third plate. The 2 sections should be next to each other.

You have shaded in 2/8 of the plate.

With the blue crayon shade in 3 sections of the plate. The 3 sections should be next to each other.

You have shaded in 3/8 of the plate.

If you pretend that the plate is a pizza pie,
it's clear that there's more pizza
in the blue section than in the green section.
And more in the green than in the red.

3/8 is more than 2/8 or 1/8.

2/8 is more than 1/8.

What happens to a fraction as the numerator,
the top number, gets larger?

As the numerator gets larger the fraction gets larger.

Now that you know about fractions,
you can find the weight of some things
that weigh almost nothing at all.

You can find the weight of a penny,
a nickel, or a dime.

To weigh them you will need:

a scale like a diet or postage scale, a scale that will register as little as one ounce.

You will also need a lot of pennies, nickels, and dimes.

How much does a penny weigh?

If you put one penny on the scale it seems to weigh nothing at all.

Add a penny.

Keep adding pennies until the scale registers one ounce.

How many pennies did it take?

Take the pennies off the scale and do the same thing with nickels.

Take the nickels off the scale and do the same thing with dimes.

How much does each penny, nickel, or dime weigh?

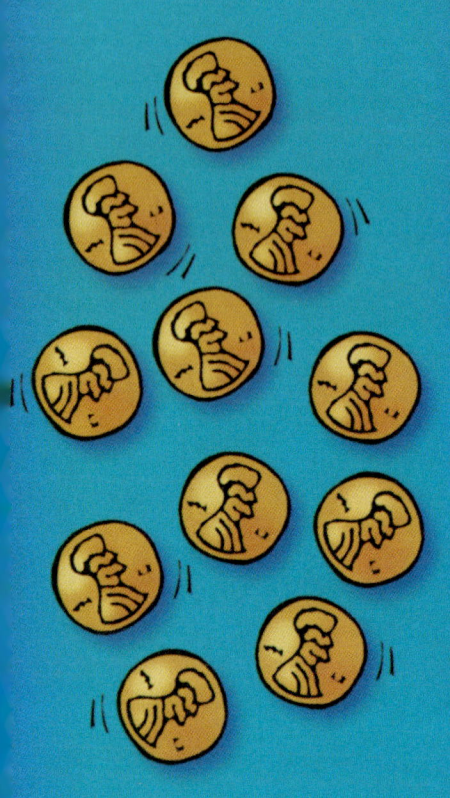

On my scale, 11 pennies together weighed one ounce.

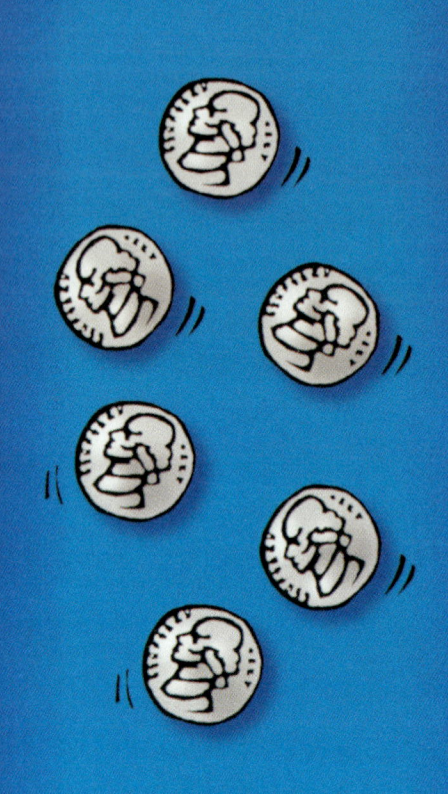

6 nickels weighed one ounce.

13 dimes weighed one ounce.

$\frac{1}{11}$

$\frac{1}{6}$

$\frac{1}{13}$

Each penny weighs 1/11 of an ounce.

Each nickel weighs 1/6 of an ounce.

Each dime weighs 1/13 of an ounce.

Which coin weighs the most?

The nickel is the heaviest of the three coins.
The smaller the bottom number of a fraction,
the denominator, the larger the fraction.

1/6 is more than 1/11 or 1/13.

Which coin weighs the least?

The dime is the lightest coin.
The larger the bottom number of a fraction,
the denominator, the smaller the fraction.

1/13 is less than 1/11 or 1/6.

Now get some:

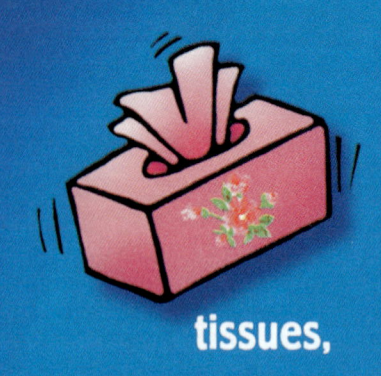

tissues, envelopes, and pencils.

How much does each tissue weigh?

If you put just one tissue on the scale
it seems to weigh nothing at all.
Keep adding tissues until the scale registers one ounce.

How many tissues together weigh one ounce?
That number is your denominator.

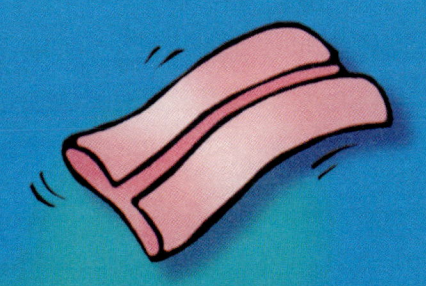

How much does each tissue weigh?

How much does each envelope weigh?

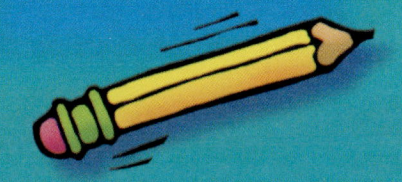

How much does each pencil weigh?

Which weighs the most,
a tissue, an envelope, or a pencil?

Which weighs the least?

Sometimes it's hard to tell
if one fraction is more or less than another.
Sometimes, even though two fractions look different,
with different numerators and denominators,
they are really the same.

To learn about fractions that look different
but are really the same, you will need:

Graph paper, **a pencil,** **a ruler,** **and a crayon.**

**Using your ruler,
draw three rectangles on the graph paper.
Make each rectangle the same size,
four boxes long and two boxes wide.**

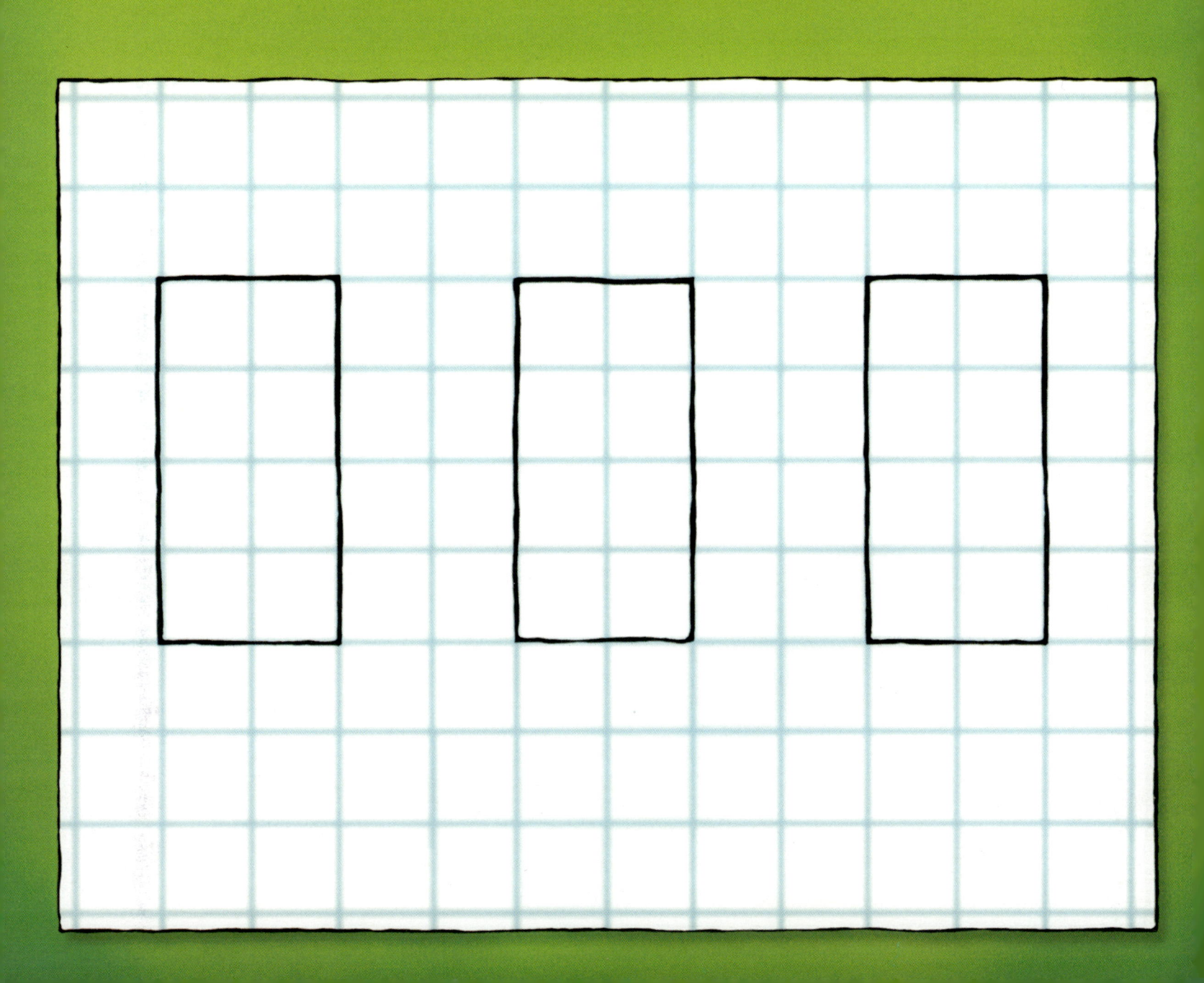

Divide the first rectangle into 2 equal parts, into 1/2s. With a crayon shade in 1/2 of the first rectangle.

Divide the second rectangle into 4 equal parts, 1/4s. Shade in 2/4 of the second rectangle.

Divide the third rectangle into 8 equal parts, 1/8s. Shade in 4/8 of the third rectangle.

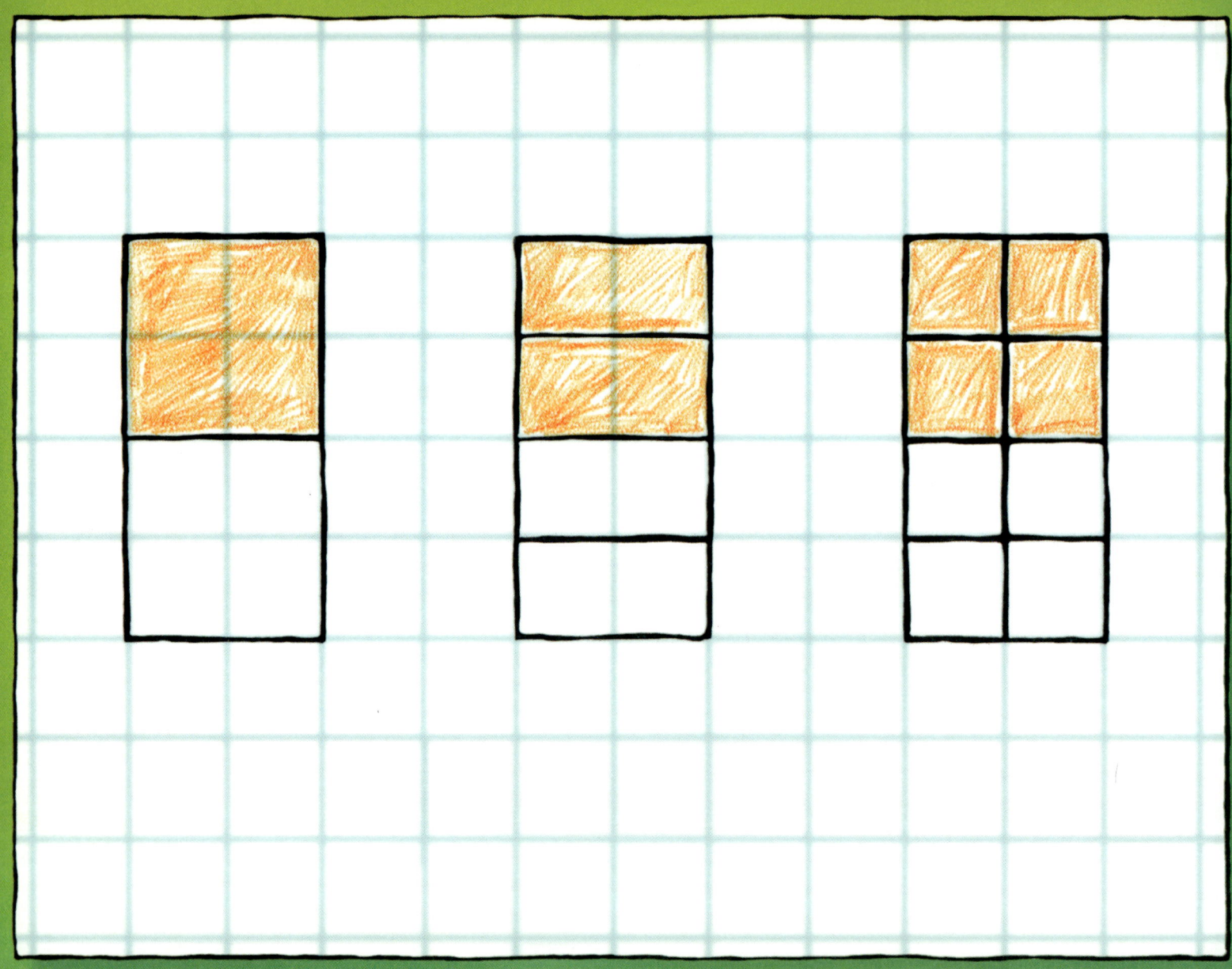

Compare the shaded sections of each rectangle. They should look the same.

1/2, 2/4, and 4/8 are equal fractions.

Coins can also teach you about fractions.

=

There are 4 quarters in a dollar.
Each quarter is 1/4 of a dollar.

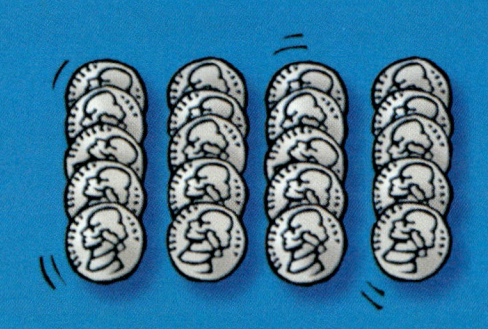

=

There are 20 nickels in a dollar.
Each nickel is 1/20 of a dollar.

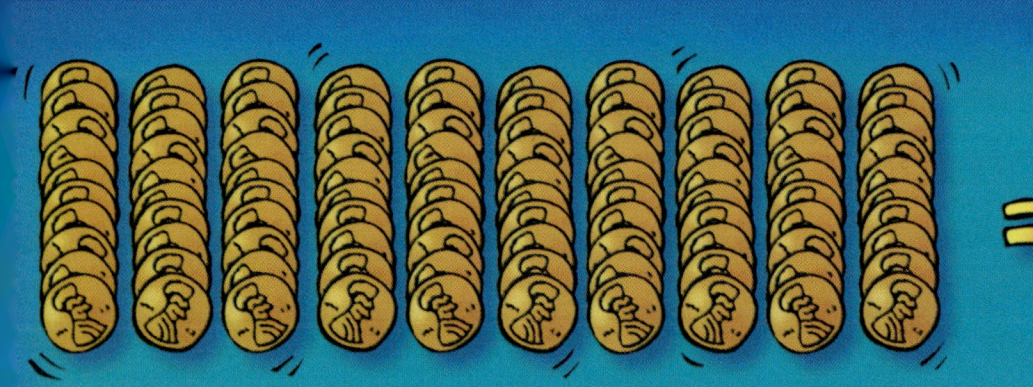

=

There are 100 pennies in a dollar.
Each penny is 1/100 of a dollar.

1 quarter is 1/4 of a dollar.
It's 25 cents.

5 nickels are 5/20 of a dollar.
They're 25 cents.

25 pennies are 25/100 of a dollar.
They're 25 cents, too.

1/4, 5/20, 25/100 are equal fractions. There are lots of other equal fractions.

Now that you know about fractions,
start looking for them.

When a glass is only partly filled with juice,
only a fraction of the glass is filled.

When you have read one of many chapters in a book, you have read only a part, just a fraction, of the book.

Keep on the lookout for fractions.

They're everywhere.